PORTSMOUTH
IN OLD PHOTOGRAPHS

PORTSMOUTH
IN OLD PHOTOGRAPHS

COLLECTED BY
PETER N. ROGERS AND DAVID F. FRANCIS

ALAN SUTTON
1989

Alan Sutton Publishing
Gloucester

First published 1989

British Library Cataloguing in Publication Data

Portsmouth in old photographs.
1. Hampshire. Portsmouth, history
I. Rogers, Peter
942.2'792

ISBN 0-86299-685-6

Typesetting and origination by
Alan Sutton Publishing.
Printed in Great Britain by
Dotesios Printers Limited.

CONTENTS

INTRODUCTION

The Portsmouth City Records Office is greatly indebted to the authors of this book, Peter Rogers and David Francis, who have most generously agreed to donate all profits from the venture to the Friends of the Portsmouth City Records Office. Established in 1975, the 'Friends' exist primarily to stimulate public interest and to encourage public involvement in the work of the City Records Office. Among other aims they provide, where appropriate, financial assistance for the improvement of the public services of the City Records Office and for the purchase of books, documents and technical equipment. Over the years, our 'Friends' have provided us with a number of pieces of equipment, most notably a lectern for public meetings, a slide projector and screen and ultra-violet lamps, and have also purchased several significant books and documents at auction. The profits from the sale of this book will assist them in this work and the general public will be the beneficiaries.

This collection of old photographs joins a distinguished line of similar publications which have appeared in recent years including an earlier volume published by Peter and David, *Portsmouth in old Picture Postcards* (1985) and by Peter, *Cosham with Widley and Hilsea in old Picture Postcards* (1986).

What is the fascination with old photographs? Why do published collections of old pictures sell so well? Why, indeed, is the study of local history fast overtaking gardening as the most popular national pastime? Is it purely nostalgia for what is perceived in the hurly-burly of today as an uncomplicated and romantic past? Or is it symptomatic of some deeper national malaise? Perhaps we simply have more leisure time in which to indulge our passions and interest; and old photographs and picture postcards are fascinating to study. They are instant visual history. Each picture tells a story and, as the old adage says, every picture is worth a thousand words. This is also an age which stresses the importance of the visual image, sometimes almost to the exclusion of the spoken or written word! Finally, it is also worth recalling that until comparatively recently, old picture postcards were still within the price range of the average collector. It is probably true to say that most people have in their possession a handful of old views of their home town. In fact, A.W. Coysh in *The Dictionary of Picture Postcards in Britain 1894–1939* (1984) suggests that during the first decade of this century nearly every family had an album of cards, which besides being a cheap form of communication before the days of the telephone, were attractive items in their own right. Whatever the reason for their popularity, it is an undisputed fact that published collections of pictures will always find a market today.

In addition to our collections of photographs, we have nearly four thousand original picture postcards in the City Records Office. Some two thousand of these views are of Portsmouth and its immediate hinterland. The rest cover south-east Hampshire, the Isle of Wight and the rest of the United Kingdom. A small group of some two hundred cards covers every possible subject, including actors and actresses, humorous subjects, and advertising material. Almost two thousand of the cards are printed, in either black and white or in colour. The rest are original photographs, mostly black and white. Many of them belong exclusively to the City Records Office to which Peter and David have had access. The other cards have been deposited on long-term loan by their owners and are available for study in our Search Room.

By their very nature, picture postcards are vulnerable to loss and damage. They are small (usually $5\frac{1}{2} \times 3\frac{1}{2}$ in) can be misplaced easily and, sad to say, readily purloined. They are also liable to become dog-eared if handled too frequently and, if they are original photographs, the image itself is likely to deteriorate with age. As custodians of a large collection of picture postcards, we are very much aware of these different problems and a programme of conservation has begun. Each card will be conserved, as necessary, by our conservation staff, mounted, put in a clear sleeve and appropriately stored in optimum conditions in either our Strong Rooms or newly-equipped Photographic Store. This programme will cost money – almost £1.00 a card. We propose asking the Friends of the Portsmouth City Records Office to put the monies raised by the sale of this book towards the cost of this conservation programme. I would therefore urge you – and your friends and relatives – to purchase as many copies of this book as possible and thus underwrite a most desirable cause.

Sarah Quail
Portsmouth City Records Office
June 1989.

Portsmouth at Worship

PRIDE OF PLACE among the churches of Portsmouth must go to St Mary's, Portsea. It is our largest and most impressive, and has the oldest foundation, dating from c. 1164. The present building was begun in 1887 and consecrated in 1889. W.H. Smith, the bookseller, member of parliament and First Lord of the Admiralty, caricatured as Sir Joseph Porter in the Portsmouth-set Gilbert and Sullivan opera *HMS Pinafore*, provided most of the funds (see M. Sparrow, *One Hundred Not Out*, Portsmouth, St Faith's Centre, 1980, appendix 5).

THE MEDIEVAL CHURCH of St Mary lasted until 1843, when it was replaced by the one in the centre of this composite view. This was constructed to the design of Thomas Ellis Owen, better remembered for many fashionable villas in Southsea. For some reason, the original medieval tower was retained.

St Marys Church Kingston Portsmouth 18... with old original Tower

THIS LARGER VIEW of the second St Mary's shows the mass of tombstones that once surrounded it, and graphically indicates why St Mary's Road used to be known as Dead Man's Lane. Rapid population growth in the area in the mid-nineteenth century soon outstripped the church's capacity; hence its replacement after less than 50 years.

Below, right.
EIGHT OF ST THOMAS' TEN BELLS were originally cast in 1703 and were a gift from Admiral Sir George Rooke, then the MP for Portsmouth. Persistent stories that they had once hung in Dover Castle and were a gift from Prince George of Denmark can be discounted, for the Dover bells remained there until 1779. This picture was taken in 1912, prior to a complete recasting. In 1957 a further two bells were added to the tower, so completing the present peal of ten.

WHAT IS NOW PORTSMOUTH'S (ANGLICAN) CATHEDRAL was a daughter church of St Mary's from its consecration in 1185 until 1320, when it became Portsmouth's parish church. It was raised to the dignity of a cathedral to serve the newly founded Anglican diocese in 1927 and considerably extended but, at the time of writing (1989), completion plans are still to be implemented. This was the first church in England to be dedicated to St Thomas of Canterbury.

ST THOMAS' had a chapel of ease from 1839 to 1921. Dedicated to St Mary, it stood some 100 yards west of where Highbury Street, (then St Mary's Street) now ends, on a site subsequently engulfed by Portsmouth power station. This was in turn demolished by 1984, and a housing development now occupies the site.

A DISSENTING MEETING-HOUSE or chapel had been built in Penny Street in 1691. The congregation moved to the building illustrated, in High Street, after its completion in 1718 or 1719. They became avowedly Unitarian in 1819. The chapel was partially restored in 1822 but then remained, externally at least, virtually unaltered until a Nazi bomb wrecked it on 10 January 1941. Happily, a replacement chapel was built.

REVD JOHN KNAPP was one of the many clergymen to whom residents of the less fashionable parts of our town had cause to be grateful. He was minister of St John's from 1853 to 1881, and also founded the Circus Church.

ST JOHN'S stood in Prince George's Street (just north of Queen Street). It was opened by the Bishop of Winchester on 31 July 1789 as a proprietary chapel, deriving its income entirely from pew rents; indeed, it was only in 1835 that it gained a parish. St John's was destroyed in an air raid on 12 August 1940.

ST JOHN'S was designed by Nicholas Vass in the florid Venetian style prevalent at the time. It was a 'Protestant Temple', with the communion table in the apse and a three-decker pulpit, which was subsequently replaced by a separate pulpit, reading desk and lectern.

REVD KNAPP gained his appointment as a result of a preaching contest and, like all other ministers who served at St John's, he was an ardent Evangelical. Seeking to spread the word, he lighted upon a disused circus building on the corner of Lion Gate (now Edinburgh) Road and Fountain Street in 1857, to use for religious purposes. He had the support of the vicar of Portsmouth (in whose parish the building stood) and the first service took place on 7 June 1857.

THE FORMER CIRCUS, 'so long the scene of folly, licentiousness and sin, resounded with the melody of prayer and praise' from congregations often numbering over 2,000. Revd Knapp was joined in his labours there by Revd John Martin in 1859.

THE OLD CIRCUS CHURCH soon became unsafe and this new church was opened in Surrey Street on 28 December 1864.

HERE IS THE INTERIOR OF THE NEW CHURCH at its opening, with its conspicuously enormous double-decker pulpit, (a victory for the architect over the incumbent). This was eventually demolished c. 1920, and the whole interior was refurbished in the church's diamond jubilee year (1924). The church was blitzed on 10 January 1941, although worship continued there until 1951, when special closing services were held on 25 and 28 February.

FINALLY, we see a group of pupils from the Circus Church School. The date is uncertain, the number 14 probably refers to the class. The two interior views shown earlier are believed to date from 1864, when the old church closed and the new one opened; this photograph was found in the same collection so it may even date from that time.

KENT STREET BAPTIST CHAPEL had its origins in a congregation at Forton who decided to meet in Portsea to avoid the inconvenience of crossing the harbour. Their original building (1704), in what was then known as Meeting-House Alley, was built with material from the ruined Netley Abbey. The chapel needed continuous improvement and enlarging so a new building, seating nearly 800 people, was opened in September 1847. This was badly damaged by fire in 1891 but was rebuilt, only to become another victim of the air raid of 10 January 1941.

HERE IS AN INTERIOR VIEW of the chapel, with members of the congregation sitting around the organ.

ST GEORGE'S CHURCH was built in 1753–54 at the instigation of local people who complained, with some justification, that the walk to their parish church (St Mary's, Portsea) was too long. This area was once one of the more fashionable parts of Portsea, and a pleasant description of the church (disguised as St Faith's) and its congregation features in the novel *By Celia's Arbour*, by Portsmouth-born author Sir Walter Besant.

HERE WE SEE THE CHURCH OF ST MICHAEL AND ALL ANGELS, which stood on the south-east corner of Park Road (now King Henry I Street) and St Michael's Road, approximately where the Polytechnic's St Michael's Building is now located. The church had its origins in a mission established in White's Row (one of the most notorious streets in Portsea) by Revd Reginald Shutte, a curate of Holy Trinity, in 1865. The church sustained some bomb damage in 1941, but was able to take on the role of chapel to the Royal Naval barracks after the virtual destruction of Holy Trinity the same year. St Michael's was finally demolished in 1960.

THE EBENEZER BAPTIST CHAPEL in Castle Road was the first place of worship on Southsea Common, opening on 22 January 1809. In 1891, a splinter group from the Kent Street Chapel formed themselves into the Immanuel Baptists, and joined with the Ebenezer congregation. This led to overcrowding and a new chapel was built in Victoria Road, rendering the one illustrated redundant by 1899.

CONGREGATIONAL WORSHIP in Victoria Road began in 1883. This iron church was erected c. 1888, to be replaced in 1911 by the building which still stands.

AS A RESULT of a reaction by the Church of England to the spread of nonconformity in Portsmouth around the turn of the eighteenth and nineteenth centuries, All Saints' and St Paul's churches (illustrated here) were built. St Paul's Square, east of Hampshire Terrace, was its location. The church was consecrated in October 1822, and served its district until March 1941, when it was bombed and burnt out. The shell survived until 1959, when it was finally demolished.

HERE WE SEE ST BARTHOLOMEW'S CHURCH in Outram Road, its site commemorated today by the housing development called St Bartholomew's Gardens. It was consecrated on 1 December 1864. Finances for its upkeep were rarely plentiful and, by the early 1950s, it was in such a precarious state that the cheapest means of providing a church in the area was to rebuild the blitzed St Matthew's (off Fawcett Road) and combine the two parishes under the new name of the Holy Spirit. The last service at St Bartholomew's was on 15 January 1958, after which it was closed and demolished.

MILTON, as will be shown later in this book, was the last separate village on Portsea Island. By 1841, there was sufficient population to warrant the construction of a church and St James', in Milton Road, was consecrated on 30 September that year.

HERE IS A RARE VIEW of St James' from the east, overlooking the fields. Population growth eventually overtook the church's 200 seat capacity and the present St James', unusually running north–south, was consecrated on 25 July 1913, the original church passing into memory.

ST PATRICK'S CHURCH, in Eastfield Road, is a daughter church of St James', built in 1906 to the design of G.E. Smith, the borough architect. This photograph, taken before the halls were added, gives a rare view of the west end which hasn't been possible since. Curiously, the altar is located at this end, making what is the west end, geographically, arguably the east end ecclesiastically.

HERE IS A GROUP OF PEOPLE of St Patrick's, perhaps taken at the time of the church's opening.

THE GARRISON CHURCH in Old Portsmouth had its origins in a chapel serving the Domus Dei Hospital, founded in or around 1212. By the seventeenth century, this had been extended to become a residence for the Governors of Portsmouth. The motley collection of buildings had been demolished, and the chapel extensively rebuilt by the 1860s to serve as a church for Portsmouth's substantial garrison. Bombed on 10 January 1941, it now stands roofless as an ancient monument.

Hilsea. The Church and Pond

ST BARBARA is the patron saint of gunners (deriving from her protection for those threatened by thunderstorms or fire) and this church, dedicated to her, was built at Hilsea Barracks in 1888 as the garrison church for the Royal Artillery. The military finally left Hilsea in the early 1960s and the development known as Gatcombe Park now occupies the site.

Military and Naval Impressions

THE 'CRINOLINE' CHURCH was built as a hospital for the Crimean Campaign. On its return to England it did duty for St Bartholomew's and St Simon's until the permanent churches were built. It was then purchased by the Admiralty for use as the church of the Portsmouth Division of the Royal Marine Artillery.

THIS SUNDIAL MARKS THE SITE OF THE OLD 'CRINOLINE' CHURCH WHICH WAS BUILT AS A HOSPITAL FOR THE CRIMEA, AFTER BEING BROUGHT TO ENGLAND IT WAS PURCHASED BY THE ADMIRALTY, ERECTED AT EASTNEY AND ACCOMMODATED 900. IN 1905 THE CHURCH OF ST. ANDREW'S TOOK ITS PLACE

THE PEDESTAL, now depleted of its dial and gnomon, stands in a neglected garden plot adjacent to the Royal Marines' Barracks at Eastney. The Royal Marines' church of St Andrew, dedicated in 1905 and built of local Rowlands Castle bricks, has accommodation for 1,000 people. Since the run down of the Portsmouth Division and the closure of much of the barracks, the church is now used on only a few occasions each year.

PORTSMOUTH HAS A LONG, HAPPY AND PROUD ASSOCIATION with the Royal Marines. The regular Sunday church parades at Eastney were a spectacle which always drew crowds of enthusiastic onlookers. Compulsory church attendance of HM Services was finally discontinued in 1946.

A BIRD'S EYE VIEW of the barracks shows the parade ground and lawns which are fronted on the seaward side by fortifications built into concealed earth banks. It is probable that Henry VIII's Eastney Fort East and Eastney Fort West were originally sited here.

The Colonnade, Eastney Barracks.

THIS PHOTOGRAPH shows one of the many fine buildings which helped to make Eastney Barracks a showpiece among the local service establishments.

CAPTIONED 'Our First Guard at Eastney', the photograph is of recruits new to the Corps being inspected by their NCO outside the guard house, which is located immediately inside the main gate.

A BARRACK ROOM, typical of the period c. 1910, shows 'the apple pie' order in which bedding and equipment were habitually laid out for display.

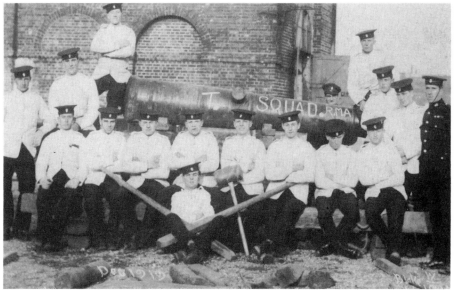

UNTIL THE AMALGAMATION in 1923 of the two Royal Marine Regiments, Eastney Barracks and Fort Cumberland were home to the Royal Marine Artillery, (the Royal Marine Light Infantry being based at nearby Gosport). Our picture shows men of the RMA relaxing during exercises at Fort Cumberland.

THE SCENE is again of men training at Fort Cumberland.

A SAD OCCASION for the Royal Marines — the funeral cortège of a late colleague, Colour Sergeant G.F. Norman, leaves the gates of the barracks *en route* for the local cemetery. (Following the Second World War, the twin gates seen here were removed, leaving one wide entrance.)

FOR CENTURIES Portsmouth was a garrison town and could number at least ten barracks. The photograph shows part of the largest complex, which included Cambridge, Clarence and Victoria barracks.

HERE WE SEE the changing of the guard at the main gate of Victoria Barracks, dated 1927. Today the site is that of the Crest Hotel which faces Pembroke Gardens in Southsea.

THE TRADITIONAL LOCATION of the saluting platform lies beyond the grass earthworks and adjacent to the ancient Square Tower. In the 1920s and 1930s, however, official salutes to visiting royalty and VIPs were fired from this position near the Garrison Church (seen on the extreme right of the photograph). With the post-war departure of the military from Portsmouth, such salutes now take place from the Gosport side of the harbour entrance.

MEN OF THE ROYAL ARTILLERY, headed by their regimental band, are pictured in Penny Street *en route* to the Garrison Church where they attended Sunday service, around 1910.

ON WHAT IS OBVIOUSLY A SPECIAL OCCASION in June 1912, the 6th Hampshire Regiment is making its way to St Thomas' and not the usual venue of the Garrison Church. Note the motor car displaying one of the earliest of Portsmouth's number plates, BK34.

THE PORTSMOUTH GARRISON was manned by various army units at different times. Here, in July 1907, are members of the sergeants' mess of the Royal Garrison Artillery.

ANOTHER MILITARY OCCASION, this time at the regimental sports of the 1st Dorset Regiment in 1908.

A REGULAR FEATURE of life in Portsmouth was the annual King's Birthday Parade, the king at this time being Edward VII and the year 1908.

THE OCCASION IN 1932, when the City of Portsmouth granted the Hampshire Regiment the Freedom of the City. The Lord Mayor is seen making his address to the troops. This was followed by a march past of the regiment exercising their newly gained right of 'marching with fixed bayonets' – a privilege granted only to those units which have been given the Freedom of the City.

MORE MEN ON THE MARCH – this time, seamen from HMS Excellent, Whale Island, crossing the bridge which will take them on to Portsea Island.

DISPLAYING THE SAME PRECISE UNIFORMITY of the Royal Marines' barrack room in a previous photograph, this scene is of a seamen's barrack room at HMS Excellent; note the rum tub in the foreground and the absence of hammocks.

AN EXPECTED AND TRADITIONAL VIEW of naval life is a seamen's mess in the Royal Naval Barracks, Portsmouth, with wooden deck, mess tables and benches, rum tubs a-plenty, hammock hooks above head level and hammocks stowed tidily in their racks. The mess utensils, bright and clean, are laid out as for inspection.

WHILE MEALS WERE served and eaten on the mess decks, the food was prepared and cooked in the establishment's galleys, a section of which is seen here. The utensils displayed in the previous photograph were the means of conveying the meals from galley to mess deck.

THE ROYAL NAVAL BARRACKS, opened in 1903, were built on the site of the earlier Anglesey Barracks, which had been an army establishment. Within the new barracks, many up-to-date and innovative features were introduced, including the canteen and concert hall. These premises were later to be involved in an incident which is described on pages 43 & 44.

The Naval Barracks, Portsmouth.

THE MAIN ENTRANCE to the Royal Naval Barracks witnessed the daily comings and goings of almost all the men who were at sometime in the Portsmouth Division. 'Baggage parties', bringing into the barracks the kitbags, hammocks, etc. were a familiar sight.

PRIOR TO THE PROVISION of a purpose-built barracks for men of the Royal Navy, the seamen had been quartered in accommodation vessels within the dockyard. These included HMS *Asia, Marlborough, Hannibal, Duke of Wellington* etc., collectively known as the 'General Depot'. The photograph shows men from those old hulks parading for an admiralty inspection, probably before the mass transfer to new quarters in RNB.

A SOURCE OF PRIDE in the new barracks was the splendid Guard House which itself was watched over by the ever vigilant lion on its roof.

NEW NAVAL BARRACKS, OFFICERS QUARTERS, PORTSEA.

FACING THE BARRACKS from across the road are the wardroom and officers' quarters. There had earlier been a military hospital on the site which was the subject of an unusual deal between the War Office and the Admiralty. When the Admiralty declared an interest in the site as a location for their officer accommodation, the War Office agreed to accept alternative land at Portsdown, where they later built the Queen Alexandra Military Hospital.

AN UNHAPPY INCIDENT, which marred the early history of the RNB, took place in November 1906, when rebellious stokers refused to accept an order given while parading for 'evening quarters'. The order, given by Lieut. B. St George Collard, was 'On the Knee' – a command used generally during gunnery exercise. The stokers resented the order and at first refused to comply. They were, it was asserted, led by Stoker Moody who was later court-martialled for inciting riotous behaviour. During that and the following evening and night, large numbers of disgruntled sailors wrecked the canteen (pictured earlier in this book) and, together with raging mobs which had gathered in the streets outside, stoned and smashed almost all the windows in the officers' quarters.

" Morning Leader" Cartoon.

ON HIS KNEES AT LAST.

[The court-martial sitting on board H.M.S. Victory found Stoker Moody guilty on two of four of the charges against him in connection with the recent riots (the outcome of the refusal to obey the order "On the knee !"), and sentenced him to five years' penal servitude.]

STOKER MOODY was, as a result of his court martial, sentenced to five years' detention. An appeal was considered and his sentence later reduced to three years. The press of the time had a field-day with the news, local and national dailies making the most of the incident. Picture postcards appeared for sale on the streets immediately following each pronouncement. The inclusion of a dog in the picture was a reference to an earlier event in the career of Lieut. Collard when, in 1905, he is alleged to have used the order 'On your knee you dog', or even, 'you dirty dog' to Stoker Albert Acton. Several months after this incident, Stoker Acton deserted from his ship, HMS *Duncan* and was never apprehended.

THE SCENE IS THE PARADE GROUND in RNB where sailors are being subjected to the rigours of yet another session of 'square bashing', a monotonous and often unnecessary form of disciplined training in 1917.

THE NAVY OPENED ITS GYMNASIUM, lecture rooms and swimming pool in nearby Pitt Street in 1910. The photograph shows sailors, covering their embarrassment if nothing else, while learning to swim.

THE ORIGINS OF HM GUNWHARF were in an establishment which was built in Portsea as early as 1662. Weapons of all types were issued, maintained and refurbished in the extensive armouries which served both the military and the Royal Navy for more than 280 years.

Portsmouth, the Old Town

PORTSMOUTH FROM AEROPLANE

COPYRIGHT
HUMPHRIES' AERIAL

THE USE OF A MAGNIFYING GLASS will reveal the wealth of detail that this photograph contains. Surprisingly, the date is pre-1921 and the diligent reader will discover the White Hart Barracks, St Mary's Church (which only had a brief existence), Victoria Pier and the construction of the new promenade fronting the Long Curtain Moat.

Bottom, right.
THE POST OFFICE at No. 89 High Street, destroyed in the bombing during the Second World War, was the general post office for the town until the building of the new GPO in Commercial Road in 1883. Dating from 1858, these premises replaced an earlier post office which had been sited in nearby Green Road. An illustrated guide to the High Street dated 1842 reveals an extant building which is almost certainly one and the same as that seen in this photograph. Lacking any further evidence, we can only assume the building to have served a different purpose prior to its use as the town post office.

DATED AROUND THE TURN OF THE CENTURY, the picture is of the High Street, when it was the commercial and business centre of the old town. Bankers, lawyers, doctors and publishers all conducted their dealings from here as did the merchants who provided for the needs of the local gentry. The horse-tram is on a route into Broad Street where there was a depot and stables.

The Museum, Portsmouth.

THE BOMBING OF THE HIGH STREET also deprived the town of its museum. The building had been opened in 1838 (the year of Queen Victoria's coronation) as the new Guildhall, replacing an ancient Town Hall which had been inconveniently located in the centre of the High Street. With the opening of our present Guildhall in 1890, these premises were thought to be an ideal situation in which to create the town museum. The bombing had left the columned façade of the building almost intact, and while present day thinking would have considered its rebuilding, it was sadly demolished to clear the way for post-war redevelopment.

ONE OF THE CITY'S MOST IMPRESSIVE VIEWS is that created by combining the Round Tower with its neighbour, Tower House. The Round Tower today remains the oldest of the Portsmouth fortifications. With origins dating from c. 1415, it was built as a protection against the French who, in 1337, 1370, 1377 and 1380, made destructive raids upon the town, burning and looting, as had the periodic raiders who ravaged our coasts almost 1,000 years earlier.

TOWER HOUSE was, until his death in 1931, the home of W.L. Wyllie RA. Wyllie was a most prolific and gifted painter of maritime scenes and landscapes, adding significantly during his lifetime to our legacy of nationally important paintings. This archway, having survived Hitler's blitz, is now all that remains of the entrance to Wyllie's studio in Broad Street. Bearing the inscription: Lat 50, Deg 47 mins, 25 secs, North: Long 1 Deg 6 mins 25 secs, West; the building was unique in the world, having no other postal address than its latitude and longitude.

STILL IN BROAD STREET, the spectacle and associated discomfort of the high tide is, from time to time, still experienced. Evidence of the precautions taken by the inhabitants can be seen at the base of many doorways, where weather boards are sometimes slotted into place to discourage the ingress of sea water. Small craft have often been known to 'sail' the length of the Broad Street.

THIS PICTURE REVEALS, all too clearly, the reason for the periodic flooding. It can be seen that Broad Street terminates at the water's edge. The ramps for the car ferries to Gosport and the Isle of Wight were located both right and left of the ferry boat and it was these ramps which encouraged the sea to enter the town. The ferry pictured is one of the steam launches which plied between Gosport and Old Portsmouth. Operated by the Floating Bridge Company, they ceased operation during the Second World War.

A CAR FERRY from the Isle of Wight disembarks its passengers at Broad Street, while a small queue of vehicles await their turn to board. Photographed in the late 1920s or early 1930s, this collection of vintage vehicles would now be the treasure of any motor museum.

UNTIL THE ESTABLISHMENT of a purpose-built fish market in Portsmouth local catches were sold, often by auction, in Bath Square. The painted wall sign on the 'Still and West' public house advertises an opening time of 4.00 a.m., an indication that, as in the great London markets, business was conducted and deals often settled before dawn in the local pubs.

KNOWN LOCALLY as a Garrison House, this sixteenth-century example is pictured on the corner of St Thomas and Highbury Streets. It was once forbidden to build houses higher than the town's defensive walls, so creating a situation where the town was invariably enveloped in a confined and low lying blanket of smoke, smog and putrid air.

THE COMMERCIAL BASIN known as the Camber, to the east of Point, has existed since earliest times. It was once much broader and shallower, and possible to ford at low tide. 'Camber' originally meant 'the part of a dockyard where cambering (i.e. bending ships' timber) is performed, and timber kept'.

A BRIDGE ACROSS THE CAMBER was built in 1842, in conjunction with deepening and extension work. That first bridge was replaced, or at least extensively repaired, and 'reopened' in 1906, to be finally removed in 1923. The Bridge Tavern perpetuates its memory.

IMPROVED MILITARY STRATEGIES, both in attack and defence, have necessitated continuous updating of Portsmouth's fortifications from the earliest times up to and including the present day. During the years 1745 to 1756, the defences of the old town were redesigned and improved to include the then latest techniques. John Peter Demaretz was the military engineer employed to plan and implement this work and, in his detailed drawing, it is interesting to note that the street pattern of the present town remains faithful to the basic grid system featured here, and indeed, in the earliest known maps of the town.

Milton, the Last Village

THE LARGEST OF OUR ISLAND VILLAGES was the last to lose its rural status. The photograph is of the junction of Milton Road with Priory Crescent.

AN IMPORTANT CENTRE OF VILLAGE LIFE, the post office, was located at this junction. The building, with modern facia, still exists today and is the office of a well-known turf accountant.

IN PRIORY CRESCENT, behind the present Milton Arms, was the local wheelwright's workshop. Surprisingly a horse can be seen receiving attention; the local farrier and blacksmith's premises were on the opposite side of the road.

DEMOLISHED IN THE EARLY 1930s, these cottages stood on the site of Milton Court, a block of flats now facing the local park.

MUCH OF MILTON PARK was originally part of Milton Farm. The farm buildings pictured here were located behind the present Public Library.

THE BARN BELONGING TO MIDDLE FARM is seen on the corner of Asylum Road (Locksway Road). A terrace of single storey shops occupies the site today.

MILTON LOCK is the most obvious visible reminder of the Portsmouth Canal which opened on 19 September 1822 as part of a route via the Arun, the Wey and connecting canals to the Thames and London. It terminated in a basin just about where Allders department store now stands. The canal could take vessels of 150 tons, but although a reasonable amount of traffic came south, return loads were always difficult to find. The owners constructed a quay near Portsbridge in 1830, with a cut to give direct access to the harbour. The canal closed in June 1831. There was one other lock 200 yds further west from that shown. The derelict Milton lock still just survives although Lime Kiln cottages also seen in the picture were demolished c. 1960.

THE 'SEA LOCK' (the largest on the London to Portsmouth waterway) is now viewed from a westerly direction with, in the foreground, the 'pound' (the basin which lay between the two Milton locks).

WHILE THE 'SEA LOCK' and pound were used as a berthing refuge by local fishermen, the inner lock was allowed to become derelict and overgrown.

FACING A PATHWAY once known locally as Common Lane, the Old Oyster House was conveniently placed for all those who walked the canal bank or who were visiting the local shore. The present Oyster House replaced the old premises in the 1930s.

TOGETHER WITH THE 'SEA LOCK', the old Engine House remains the only tangible evidence of the Portsmouth Canal. In fact there were two houses in which accommodation was provided for the lock keeper/pump operators. The lock-up garages take the place of the high canal bank, long since removed.

OPENED IN 1911 for the treatment of tubercular patients, the chalet buildings of the Langstone Sanatorium provided the fresh air conditions considered beneficial to the cure. Little protection was offered against the weather, save for half doors and tarpaulins.

A VILLAGE WITHIN A VILLAGE, the 'High Street' at Milton Locks was a community of holiday weekend chalets and houseboats, providing a haven and refuge for sailors, fishermen and city dwellers.

THE SHORELINE AT MILTON was used to berth boats and house-boats which were holiday or residential homes. Sadly, the unique character of the district was destroyed when they were forcibly removed in the late 1960s, leaving behind a derelict wilderness which remains with us 20 years later.

THE SEVERE AND MEMORABLE WINTER OF 1962/63 contributed to the Milton seascape. The ice which formed in Langstone Harbour affected the local shore when, it was claimed, it was possible to walk across the lake to the Eastney peninsula.

RETURNING TO 'COMMERCIAL' MILTON, this photograph shows the petrol filling station and caravan site which developed from Domer Farm. The original farmhouse and barn are, in fact, concealed amidst the buildings etc., of this snapshot view, dated 1960.

THE NINE ACRES of Baffins Farm were purchased in 1939 by the city for £5,500. With 'rare unanimity' the city gave an undertaking 'that the site should be preserved inviolate as long as Portsmouth lasts'.

Portsmouth on the Move

HILSEA ARCHES, part of the massive defence system which protected Portsmouth's northern shore, were removed in the early 1930s. Electric vehicles replaced the horse-trams in Portsmouth in 1901 and those serving Cosham in 1903.

PRIOR TO ITS RECONSTRUCTION in 1927, Portsbridge was of girder construction with a removable section to facilitate the passage of shipping. The hand-winding mechanism which performed the bridge separation is mounted on the centre pier.

HERE WE SEE A TRAM of the Portsdown and Horndean Light Railway at South Parade Pier. The company originally operated from Cosham to Horndean but, in later years, exercised running powers over the Corporation's tracks into Portsmouth and Southsea. The company's last service ran on 9 January 1935. Horndean trams are always distinguishable from Corporation trams, even in black and white views, from the position of their headlight, on the upper, rather than the lower deck.

THE MAY DAY PARADE of local businesses. The traditional dressing of their horses and vehicles was an annual feature of the Portsmouth carnival calendar. This entry is from Campions, a major local bakers.

THE INTRODUCTION of modern gas appliances prompted these mobile displays in the city. The steam lorry is in front of the Central Library and the motor vehicle is pictured near the Rudmore gasholder.

THE PHASING OUT of horse-drawn transport introduced another form of horsepower into the town. The photograph is of an early motorized refuse lorry.

PROBABLY PHOTOGRAPHED with a view to its advertising potential, the Portsmouth Co-operative Society proudly displays its fleet of bread delivery vans.

THE STREETS OF PORTSMOUTH were once busy with an army of errand boys delivering goods for their employers. This unusual tricycle was owned by 'A Collis, purveyor of the best meat only'.

THE SOUTHSEA CARRIAGE COMPANY operated from several addresses in the town, employing a variety of 'Horse drawn vehicles to suit any occasions'.

ANOTHER ENTRY in the May Day parade was Pickfords who had offices in Elm Grove.

H. BUNDY, TOBACCONIST, operated this graceful little vehicle providing a delivery service to his valued customers.

THE LONDON, BRIGHTON AND SOUTH COAST RAILWAY was the first to reach Portsmouth, in 1847. For many years that company had the pleasing policy of naming its locomotives after places in the area it served. Hilsea, Farlington, Cosham, Southsea (twice), Fratton (twice) and Portsmouth (twice) gave their names to engines. Our view shows the first of these, a 2–2–2 express passenger locomotive, built in 1864 by Robert Stephenson and Company. Originally there were 12 engines in its class, but four were sold back to their makers shortly afterwards for service in Egypt. *Portsmouth* was the longest serving of those that remained, surviving until the end of 1893. A new *Portsmouth*, this time an 0–4–4 tank engine, was introduced in January 1894, and survived to be taken (briefly) into British Railways ownership on nationalization in 1948, though by then it had lost its name.

FRATTON STATION opened in 1885, along with the branch line to Southsea. This had its own platforms, seen here on the right. Regular services on the Southsea branch ceased as long ago as August 1914, and the carriage washing plant now occupies the site of its platforms at Fratton.

SOUTHSEA began its resort existence as a haven for retired persons and half-pay officers but, by the 1920s, a Beach and Publicity Committee had been established, and various attractions and amusements provided. Here is an early view of the Southsea Miniature Railway.

THE CORPORATION acquired some redundant military land on the north-west of Portsea Island in 1930 and, by 1935, this had become Hilsea Lido. The Lido still exists, but the miniature railway seen here ceased operating c. 1950.

THIS SARO 'WINDHOVER' FLYING BOAT, *City of Portsmouth*, was purchased in 1932 by the Hon. Mrs Victor Bruce. Adventuress, pilot, racing driver and power-boat enthusiast, Mrs Bruce intended to capture the British flight endurance record with the aircraft. Following a disappointing first attempt she was finally successful in remaining in the air for 54 hrs and 13 mins before a fault in an oil pipe terminated the attempt in August 1932. In-flight refuelling was achieved with the aid of a Bristol fighter and a Gypsy Moth aircraft.

CHIEF CONSTABLE RECEIVE A WELCOME VISITOR FROM THE CLOUDS : M SALMETS ALIGHT ON THE COMM...

THE CAPTION ON THE PHOTOGRAPH gives no clue as to the date or reason for the 'flying visit' of M. Salmet and his landing on Southsea Common. Suffice to say perhaps, that this unusual event generated considerable local interest and involved a welcoming committee headed by Portsmouth's Chief Constable.

WITH A SURPLUS of First World War aviators and machines, markets were sought where both could be usefully employed. Portsmouth was one of the sites chosen by these flying entrepreneurs who flew pleasure flights from a location which is near the present Southsea Skate Park. Clarence Parade and Lennox Road form the background.

HYDROPLANE ARRIVING AT SOUTHSEA

HYDROPLANES OF THE ROYAL NAVAL AIR SERVICE are featured in both of these photographs. The first is seen flying off Eastney shore; the second shows a working party of Royal Marines manhandling the aircraft out of the water and up the shingle beach.

ONE OF THE EARLIEST POSTCARDS to feature aircraft at Portsmouth shows two army aeroplanes at Hilsea on a site which in later years was to become Rugby Camp. Both aircraft served with the 3rd Squadron Royal Army Flying Corps and had flown in on a training flight from the Larkhill Flying School on Salisbury Plain. The numbers displayed on the tail sections of the aircraft show them to be 286, a Henry Farman F20 and 288, an early Avro 500E.

AIRCRAFT pictured at Portsmouth Airport in September 1931, where they are gathered not as participants but as interested spectators of the Schneider Trophy Air Race. Britain won the event and retained the trophy for all time.

Borough Engineer Extraordinaire

A PERSONAGE hardly mentioned in other books on Portsmouth (Geoffrey Stavert's *A Study in Southsea* being an honourable exception) but who has left several important marks on its topography is H.P. Boulnois, who was Borough Engineer from 1883 until 1900. The following ten views draw attention to some of his achievements.

BOULNOIS FOUND A VARIETY OF MONUMENTS AND TROPHIES scattered along the beach and he rearranged them into some semblance of order. Here is a rare view, (originally stereoscopic) of the *Victory's* anchor in its original position, west of Clarence Pier.

BOULNOIS DESIGNED THE GRANITE PLINTH on which the anchor now stands, east of Clarence Pier. He originally decorated it with heavy chains round the shaft and stock, but soon had them removed when it was pointed out to him that in Nelson's time, only hawsers were used on anchors.

HERE WE SEE THE CRIMEA MEMORIAL, with veterans from that campaign proudly displaying their medals. Is it possible that any of those present was born in the eighteenth century?

Southsea Castle. 252 Copyright Edgar Ward

ONE OF BOULNOIS' FIRST UNDERTAKINGS was to construct the promenade along the length of the seafront. This necessitated these associated sea defences in front of Southsea Castle. Previously, a walk between the castle and the sea required considerable agility and was fraught with danger.

OLD SEMAPHORE TOWER, PORTSMOUTH.

THE SQUARE TOWER has had a variety of uses in its nearly 500 years of history. Boulnois obtained permission from the War Office to install a tank on top, for supplying sea water to the swimming baths and for street watering and sewage flushing. Regrettably, it has not been possible to obtain a view of this.

AT THE EASTERN END of the sea front, there was a frequent problem of shingle being blown across the promenade on to the road in stormy weather. Boulnois built the continuous wall and seat facing the sea to offset this problem. Our view dates from around 1927.

HERE IS ANOTHER VIEW of Boulnois' wall and seat in 1988. Occasionally, very bad weather still brings shingle on to the road, so we may be thankful to the wall that these occasions are now rare.

CANOE LAKE AND
SOUTH PARADE PIER, SOUTHSEA.

74

MUCH OF SOUTHSEA COMMON and the adjoining areas were a boggy morass, and the part round Craneswater a particular eyesore. Boulnois had the job of improving this by making the Canoe Lake, a task successfully completed in June 1886.

Recreation Ground, North End, Portsmouth.

The Spithead
Series. No.633.

ANOTHER OF BOULNOIS' CONTRIBUTIONS to the town was Alexandra Park, where the banked cycle track in the stadium was an innovation in its time.

THE ESPLANADE SOUTHSEA (171)

WHAT IS NOW CLARENCE ESPLANADE had its rudimentary beginnings in 1807. It was considerably improved by the efforts of Lord Frederick Fitzclarence, the Lieutenant-Governor, in 1848. Boulnois had the task of laying it out to modern standards and providing the adjacent road. This view also shows some of the neatly rearranged trophies and memorials.

Work, Leisure and Pleasure

IN THIS PARTICULARLY OLD PHOTOGRAPH (1879), we gain a glimpse of a way of life long forgotten. The premises of W.M. Wade, Gas Fitter and Paper Hanger, were situated at No. 13 Lake Road. Gas lighting had been introduced to the streets of Portsmouth in 1821 though it is not known from which year the citizens were able to enjoy the domestic benefits of lighting and cooking.

SPECIALIST PORK BUTCHERS, H. & H. Abington traded from this small shop at No. 63 Queen Street, Portsea, in the early years of this century.

THE TRADES DIRECTORY for 1906 indicates that Montague Hayes Woolley, tobacconist, was at No. 69 Queen Street, a near neighbour of the butcher's shop in the previous photograph.

BISHOP BROS., manufacturers and retailers of boots and shoes, traded from three addresses in Portsmouth and two in nearby Gosport. It was a proud and unusual boast that their sales nationwide averaged 20 tons of boots and shoes each week.

LOADER'S TEMPERANCE DINING ROOM, the working man's cafe of the day, was pleased to advertise that, 'Everything was as nice as mother made it.'

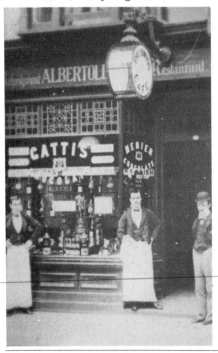

THE SWISS CAFÉ PREMISES of the brothers Albertolli occupied a prime site on the corner of Edinburgh Road and the Arcade. Another restaurant owned by the family, the Continental Café, was located south of the Theatre Royal.

OLDER RESIDENTS will recall that, for most of their lives, W. Pink & Sons were Portsmouth's principal grocers. From small beginnings c. 1860, the company grew to be a dominant force in the trade and it was with regret that local folk witnessed the closure of the company after more than 100 years. The picture, heavily retouched, is of their early premises in Commercial Road.

W. PINK & SONS, re-established in larger premises, provided accommodation for the early Municipal Telephone Exchange which was housed in an upper storey. Opened in 1904, the exchange carried 360 local subscriber lines and 1,500 multiple field subscriber lines. The view of Commercial Road on p. 148 shows, at roof level, the massive framework housing the telephone connections.

ARTHUR CONAN DOYLE, the creator of Sherlock Holmes, was, from 1882 to 1900, a practising physician at No. 1 Bush Villas, Elm Grove, and it was here that his great detective was 'born'. In keeping with many other dwellings in Elm Grove, the house subsequently acquired a shop front and, by 1903, Madame Lee had her corset shop there.

THE ANNUAL ARRIVAL OF SANTA CLAUS at the city's major department stores is not a recent introduction. This photograph shows the 'Old Gentleman' approaching journey's end in pre-war Palmerston Road, apparently to alight at Southsea's Knight & Lee store?

THE PHOTOGRAPH reveals the existence of Price's Bedding and Furniture 'Re-furbishing' Company of Fraser Road, Southsea.

BOTH THE WALL AND GAS HOLDER were considered worthy of preservation when the Rudmore Works were closed. The wall was reckoned to be a prime example of the bricklayer's craft and the gas holder, of classic design, was seriously thought to be an admirable feature for conversion into a restaurant. Portsmouth's Ferry Port now covers the site.

WITH A CONTINUING INCREASE in demand for industrial and domestic gas, the works at Flathouse and Rudmore were considered to be inadequate and a new site was secured at Hilsea. The land surrounding the new works can be seen to be undeveloped at the time.

ONCE THE SITE of the medieval church of St Mary Colwort, the electricity generating station dominated the Highbury Street area of 'Old Portsmouth' until it was demolished. The photograph shows the conveyor which lifted sea-born coal from the colliers to the furnaces.

Theatre Royal, Commercial Road,   *Portsmouth.*

THE NEW THEATRE ROYAL (now being restored after many years of neglect) was originally opened in August 1900. It was designed by the famous theatrical architect Frank Matcham for J.W. Boughton. To minimize the time the theatre had to be closed, the external walls were erected round those of its predecessor.

Theatre Royal, Portsmouth.   THE NORTH END STUDIO, PORTSMOUTH

TO COINCIDE WITH THE OPENING, the interior was lavishly redecorated in a manner reflecting the naval and military importance of Portsmouth. Bows of ships with figureheads divided the boxes and a variety of dolphins, mermaids, anchors and lifebelts adorned the front of the dress circle.

THE HIPPODROME THEATRE was another important building lost in the blitz of 10–11 January 1941. It too was in Commercial Road (now Guildhall Walk) almost opposite the Theatre Royal. This bomb-site was Portsmouth's last, its redevelopment not beginning until 1984.

THE EMPIRE PALACE was located on the south side of Edinburgh Road, a short distance from its junction with Commercial Road. It opened in 1891, but the name changed to the Coliseum in 1913, reverting to the Empire Palace again in 1950. Its end came in 1958 and a supermarket occupied the site. This has itself now been replaced by a frozen food centre.

A GUIDE BOOK OF 1930 describes the swimming pool in children's corner, just west of Southsea Castle, as 'recently completed'. Admission was 3d. per session.

WE REFERRED BRIEFLY ON p. 76 to the origins of Hilsea Lido. Here is a view of the swimming pool in its early days.

HERE ARE TWO VIEWS of the seaside delights of Southsea of bygone days. Looking westwards towards Clarence Pier, this old postcard shows an unusual juxtaposition of First World War searchlight emplacements with, in the distance, bathing machines. They can only have existed side by side for a very short time.

NOW WE ARE EAST OF SOUTH PARADE PIER, looking eastwards. The long rows of Corporation-owned beach tents were known locally as 'the tented village'.

The Gondolas at the Venetian Fête Southsea

THE ORIGINS OF THE CANOE LAKE were touched on briefly on p. 87. In its early days, activities beyond routine boating took place, as witness this view of gondolas at a Venetian Fête. The postcard providing this view is dated September 1907; no further details are to hand and more information would be welcome.

EVEN BEFORE THE CANOE LAKE WAS FORMED, the area had been associated with wildfowl, (the name of the surrounding district, Craneswater, being attributed to this). Swans have always been associated with the lake and, in earlier times, they were encouraged by the provision of the 'swannery' illustrated.

The Bandstand, Southsea Common.

THE NATIONAL POPULARITY OF THE 'BANDSTAND' as a means of entertainment encouraged the building of several in Portsmouth and Southsea. Providing music for listening, dancing and skating, this bandstand near the 'Ladies' Mile' was the venue for many of Southsea's alfresco events.

SKATING FOR FUN at another local rendezvous. The children are positively overdressed by today's standards.

THE FIRST SOUTH PARADE PIER, shown here, was opened on 26 July 1879 by Princess Edward of Saxe-Weimar, the wife of the Lieutenant-Governor of Portsmouth. Its unsophisticated configuration of a simple deck with a bandstand and landing stages at the far end reflect the simpler pleasures acceptable in the Victorian era.

South Parade Pier on Fire, July 19th/04.

IN SPITE OF ENERGETIC CLAIMS by its proprietors that it was fireproof, the first South Parade Pier was badly damaged by fire on the afternoon of 19 July 1904.

TWO YEARS LATER, the Corporation purchased and demolished the derelict pier. It was replaced by this much grander affair in 1908, seen here with builders' ladders and scaffolding still on site. The bathing machines look as pristine as the pier itself.

NEW SOUTH PARADE PIER. BAND STAND. & PROMENADE. CRIBB 10

THE NEW PIER was formally opened on 12 August 1908, by the Mayor, Cllr F.G. Foster and his Mayoress, his young daughter Doris, seen together in the right foreground. (See also p. 124).

HERE IS A CLOSE-UP VIEW of the two turnstiles that served as entrances to the pier. The playbills in the background are reminders that the pier housed a fully-fledged theatre where top stars appeared.

SOUTH PARADE PIER AND CANOE LAKE, SOUTHSEA, AERIAL VIEW

THIS FINE AERIAL VIEW taken between the wars will bring back many memories. On the 11 June 1974, fire struck again and most of the superstructure seen here was destroyed. Happily, the present superstructure was soon provided.

HERE WE SEE THE BEGINNINGS OF CLARENCE PIER. Originally built in 1842 and known as Southsea Pier, it was reconstructed and reopened on 1 June 1861 as Clarence Pier. On the right are the buildings that became the Esplanade Hotel, here serving as assembly rooms and baths.

CLARENCE PIER'S main early role was to provide access for Isle of Wight Steamers, to which end a tramway connected it with Portsmouth and Southsea Station until the railway line was extended to the harbour in 1876. (A tram and the tracks are visible in the previous view.) The tracks still appear to be in place in this view, with what may be a signal at the entrance to the pier.

Entrance to Clarence Pier, Southsea

HERE ARE TWO MORE VIEWS of Clarence Pier showing further developments; the upper one gives a good view of the Esplanade Hotel, the lower shows an impressive clutter of advertisements on the main buildings. Clarence Pier and the Hotel were further victims of the blitz.

IN THE EARLY DAYS, the provision of some of the pleasures of being at sea without its associated discomforts was selling point enough for the seaside piers. In the Edwardian era, a simple stroll on the pier, preferably in one's best clothes, was a pleasure in itself.

12   SOUTHSEA. — On Clarence Pier. — *Arrival of the Boat.* — LL

OUR FINAL LOOK at Clarence Pier shows a twin-funnelled paddle steamer, once common around the coasts on scheduled services as well as pleasure trips. Now, apart from the annual visit from the Paddle Steamer Preservation Society's PS *Waverley*, they are but a memory in Portsmouth.

THE POPULARITY OF COACH OUTINGS was, and probably still is, a British tradition. Members of St Edmund's Guild are pictured here in 1911 enjoying a church outing when the horse-drawn brake stopped briefly on Portsdown Hill.

A VINTAGE PHOTOGRAPH dated 1888 reveals members of the Portsmouth YMCA Cycling Club at Stubbington Lodge, North End.

THE CREW OF AN ISLE OF WIGHT TO PORTSMOUTH TOW BOAT share an off duty moment with local children. Tow boats are again featured on pp. 144 and 145 of this book.

THE PRE-WAR CELEBRATION of Empire Day with military and civilian parades, provided boys of the scouting organizations with an excuse to exercise their skills on Southsea Common. Notice particularly the old style uniforms and the carrying of a staff.

BEFORE BEING DESTROYED in the Second World War bombing, the Navy Tavern had been situated on an island site between Queen Street and Half Moon Street since at least 1825, when the premises were those of a wine and spirit importer. The building at that time included a private family chapel. The Portsmouth trades directory for 1890 indicates its first use as a public house when the name was the Army and Navy Tavern. The title of Navy Tavern seems to have been adopted by 1900. The photograph, c. 1930, shows, standing in the doorway, the then landlord Mr A.S. Carter.

ONE OF THE PRINCIPAL COACHING INNS of Portsmouth before the railway era was the Blue Posts in Broad Street, whence Andrew Nance, driving the coach *Tantivi* once set a record time to London of 5 hrs and 42 mins. The inn was destroyed by fire on 7 May 1870. This is its replacement, untruthfully named the Old Blue Posts, which was sadly destroyed in the blitz.

THE DUKE OF BUCKINGHAM is still a well-known hostelry in the High Street today, but a comparatively recent replacement for the one seen here which was destroyed in the blitz. The name derives from Charles I's favourite, the Duke of Buckingham, who was assassinated in a house nearly opposite in 1628.

TAKING ITS NAME FROM AN EARLY LANDLORD, Judd's Railway Hotel occupied a prime position opposite Portsmouth's General Post Office until the post-war redevelopment of this busy junction. Sharing with the adjacent railway station the bombing of the Second World War, Judd's nevertheless remained open even though the family living accommodation was uninhabitable.

COMMERCIAL ROAD, Mile End, was the location of the Sailor's Return until the construction of the massive dual carriageway. The well-known and unique hanging sign was later transferred to another local pub, the Rudmore Cellars.

THE HEAVILY DECORATED NELSON TAVERN displayed several patriotic tributes to Lord Nelson including his portrait and famous 'Last Signal'.

NOW A PART OF INDUSTRIAL AND COMMERCIAL RUDMORE, the Ship and Castle is no longer seen in the unique setting of a quiet waterfront.

THE PENHALE ARMS, originally owned by Jewell's Brewery, was purchased by the Brickwood Company in 1899. In 1926, the premises were redesigned by Portsmouth architect A.E. Cogswell in the half-timbered style that became a hallmark of many Brickwood's houses. No longer a pub, the building still stands in Fratton Road, a next-door neighbour to the modern Bridge Shopping Centre.

THIS VIEW SHOWS THE NINE ELMS, a beerhouse (see opposite page) in Grigg Street c. 1875. Both these names had changed by the early years of the twentieth century, the beerhouse retaining its numerical connotations by becoming the Five Alls, and Grigg Street being renamed St Paul's Road. At one time, St Paul's Road accommodated a pub with the delightfully unusual name of Help the Lame Dog over the Stile.

THE BUILDING PICTURED is the second Coach and Horses public house to have occupied the site at Hilsea. The third and present Coach and Horses still dominates the junction of Copnor and London Roads and was opened in 1932.

AT ONE TIME the licensing laws allowed some establishments to sell all sorts of liquor, others just beer, and the directories distinguished carefully between pubs and beer retailers. Here is an example of the latter, in Byerley Road, Fratton. The dates when beerhouses disappeared vary from place to place; Portsmouth saw its last in 1964.

THE WARRIOR'S ARMS pictured in a neglected condition in 1939, was next-door neighbour to John Pounds' Ragged School in Highbury Street. Highbury Street, (previously St Mary's Street) was also the location of St Mary's Church which is pictured on p. 16.

Portsmouth Personalities and Places

THE 'SHELL KING', Alfred George Wilkins, is pictured in one of his shell adorned costumes. Mr Wilkins, a well-known local character, also decorated his Southsea house with examples from the local sea-shore.

A FAMILIAR FIGURE on Southsea sea front, the blind woman with her dog occupied a regular pitch in the hope of gaining a measure of charity from passers-by.

'THE ITALIAN ICE-CREAM VENDOR', a scene typical of summer days in Edwardian Portsmouth.

CAPTIONED 'SOUTHSEA'S OLDEST MILKMAN', the photograph was taken in Elm Grove in 1903.

A WAGER MADE IN 1907 prompted local blacksmith Mr W. Hayes to trundle (hand propel) these heavy wheels 1,720 miles before returning to Portsmouth in 97 days and collecting his £500 prize. On a route which included Newcastle, Carlisle, Penzance and Plymouth he was accompanied by his trainer Mr A. Elliot and a referee.

Great Trundling Feat From Portsmouth.
to Newcastle & Back in 100 Days By
W. R. Hayes.

FOLLOWING THE SUCCESS OF W. HAYES, the Ellismore brothers undertook to wheel this handcart from Portsmouth to John o'Groats and back in 100 days for a wager of £50, commencing 9 June 1910. Lacking the news coverage afforded to Mr Hayes, it has not been possible to confirm the success or failure of the venture.

IN THE SO-CALLED 'SILLY' SEASON nowadays we are able to witness the 'Bognor Birdman Rally'. In 1910, a lesser event took place when this man, known only as the 'Professor' undertook to cycle off the end of South Parade Pier!

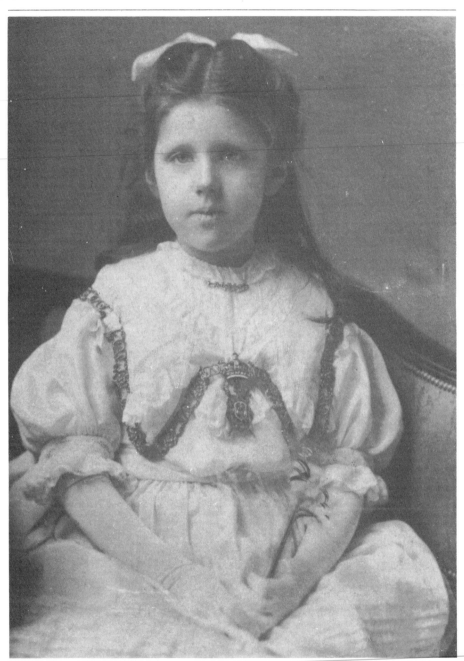

IN NOVEMBER 1907, Cllr F.G. Foster was elected Mayor of Portsmouth. As he was a widower, he was allowed to install his 5½-year-old daughter Doris as his Mayoress. It is recorded that, during her year in office, 'the little Mayoress performed her part with charming success'.

CIVIC CRICKET! On 9 June 1920 the councils of Portsmouth and Southampton played a cricket match at the Asylum Ground. The fixture was repeated on 29 June the following year at the same venue, and here we see the two mayors, Cllr J. Timpson of Portsmouth and Cllr F. Bath of Southampton, prior to leading their respective teams on to the pitch.

TO CATER FOR THE EXPANSION IN POPULATION northwards and eastwards, St Alban's Church in Copnor Road was provided. The foundation stone was laid by Princess Henry of Battenberg on 26 October 1912. The church was eventually consecrated in February 1914.

HRH THE DUKE OF YORK (later to become King George VI) unveiled Portsmouth's Naval War Memorial on 15 October 1924. This photograph shows him at the Royal Sailors' Home Club in Queen Street where, it is thought, he is meeting children who were orphaned in the First World War.

THE MARCHIONESS OF WINCHESTER, accompanied by Admiral A. Tate, Admiral Superintendent Portsmouth Dockyard, launched HMS *Orion* on 19 August 1910, 'the largest, fastest, heaviest ship set afloat at Portsmouth'.

HERE ARE MORE VIPs in Portsmouth, this time the Duke and Duchess (note the spelling mistake on the illustration) of Teck visit the Royal Counties Agricultural Show held in Southsea in June 1914. The total attendance of 78,600 broke all previous records.

"BRANKSMERE" RED CROSS HOSPITAL, SOUTHSEA.
M*** DOUGLAS SMITH (GOVERMENT HOUSE) INSTITUTED AS VICE-PRESIDENT JUNE 1918
- AND INSPECTED THE HOSPITAL, AND STAFF - PT. STEPHEN CRIBB

BRANKESMERE (sometimes spelt without the first 'e' as on the caption on both illustrations) the large house on the corner of Kent Road and Queen's Crescent was built in 1895 for the Brickwood family (the brewery magnates). During the First World War it was made available to the Red Cross as a relief hospital. These two views show events during the institution of the vice-president in June 1918. Brankesmere subsequently accommodated a girls' school, and later the police headquarters. It now houses offices of the Social Services Department.

BRANKSMERE RED CROSS HOSPITAL, SOUTHSEA. JUNE 1918
M*** DOUGLAS SMITH (GOVERMENT HOUSE) INSTITUTED AS VICE-PRESIDENT PT. STEPHEN CRIBB
AND INSPECTED

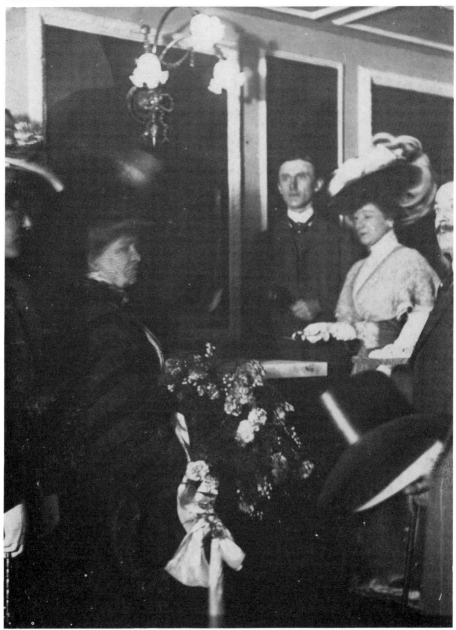

ONE OF THE COUNTRY'S LEADING COMEDIENNES, Miss Marie Tempest (1864–1942), visited Portsmouth on 17 May 1907 to formally open the Hippodrome (see also p. 99). After the ceremony, the invited audience of 1,000 watched a typical music-hall show.

JEAN BATTEN WAS INVITED to visit the recently modernized Landport Drapery Bazaar in May 1938. Our photograph shows her with the Civic welcoming party and directors of the store. Jean Batten, a New Zealander by birth, was for many years the most adventurous and successful of the world's aviators. Though considerably wealthy, she died unrecognized and forgotten in Majorca on 23 November 1982 and, because she was unknown at that time to the local authorities, lies buried in an unmarked, pauper's grave.

GIRLS SECONDARY SCHOOL, STONE LAYING —
BY MISS DAISY COUZENS —

HERE IS ANOTHER EXAMPLE of foundation stone laying, this time of the Girls' Secondary School in Fawcett Road. The date is 17 July 1906 and doing the honours is Miss Daisy Couzens, daughter of the Mayor, Sir George Couzens. She was standing in for her mother, the Mayoress, who was ill.

THE SCHOOL WAS COMPLETED the following year, and its average roll in its early days was around 400. This school was not alone in Portsmouth in having some playground space on its roof.

The Higher Grade School, Portsmouth.

THIS BUILDING STARTED LIFE as the Higher Grade School in 1892. Located in Victoria Road North, it became the Southern Secondary School in 1904. It was bombed on the evening of 10 January 1941, and after the war the school moved to Highland Road.

A WINCHESTER DIOCESAN BOARD OF EDUCATION was set up in 1838. Among its responsibilities was the founding and supporting of commercial schools, including one in Portsea. This role was taken over in 1870 by the Hampshire Diocesan Society, so it was while the school was under its aegis that this view was taken in 1875. After more changes of name, the role of the Society was assumed by the Portsmouth Diocesan Board of Finance following the setting up of the separate diocese in 1927.

A BENEFICIAL SOCIETY was founded in 1754 in Portsea for 'mutual assistance ..., and to establish a fund from which relief might be obtained'. It set up this school in Kent Street in 1784; the school itself was on the ground floor, and the Society's rooms were on the upper. This is one of the few old buildings to survive in Portsea.

THE ROYAL SEAMEN AND MARINES' ORPHAN HOME began its existence in St George's Square in 1834, moved to Lion Terrace in 1851, and finally took up residence in the premises illustrated in St Michael's Road in 1876. The buildings survived the blitz to become a Military Families' Hostel, but now King Richard I Road cuts across the site.

THE SCHOOLS WITHIN THE ROYAL MARINES' BARRACKS at Eastney were used by boys and men of the RM Division and also the sons and daughters of the Marines. Opened in 1867, the schools became eligible for an educational grant in 1894, so placing them under inspection by the Local Authority. In 1921 the Education Authorities forced the Admiralty to close the schools to children. After this date, only serving Marines and Musicians received instruction there.

THE BELL SCHOOL, built c. 1812, was so named after its connection with Andrew Bell and the National School Society. Purchased by Father Dolling in 1889, it assumed the name of Dolling's Church and thereafter was known as St Agatha's. Conservationists have fought to save the premises in Clarence Street and a compromise seems to have been reached: the façade of the old building, suitably cleaned and refurbished, has been sympathetically retained in a new building scheme.

A DAY TRAINING COLLEGE for teachers was established in Portsmouth in 1907. The first student hostels were at Ravenscourt in Elm Grove, and Ermington in Victoria Road. By Easter 1916 the purpose-built hostel (now known as Foster Hall) in Locksway Road was partially in use. These students were pictured outside just over a year later.

HERE IS A TYPICAL SCHOOL PHOTOGRAPH of the Victorian era – a class of mixed infants from Albert Road School in 1877.

Queen Street. *Portsea.*

PORTSEA developed in the early eighteenth century as an 'overspill' town for Old Portsmouth and, in its early days, Queen Street was the fashionable shopping street. In later years, Queen Street became more 'lively' than fashionable.

THIS BUILDING IN QUEEN STREET, apparently while undergoing repairs, suffered a collapse of its front wall together with the wooden scaffolding which was placed against it. Nothing is known of the incident, although the premises were thought to be those of The Shipwrecked Fishermen and Mariners' Society.

WHAT, UNTIL RECENTLY, was known as the Main Gate to the naval base was erected in the reign of Queen Anne. This view from the early years of the century recalls a time when bicycles were not allowed in, the crowd of pedestrians here providing a sharp contrast with the mass of cyclists to be seen at out-muster more recently.

THIS VIEW OF THE OLD MAIN GATE shows decorations put up evidently in anticipation of the signing of the Treaty of Versailles on 29 July 1919.

UNICORN GATE was one of the two original gates of Portsea. Erected c. 1778 at the end of North Street, it was removed to its present position c. 1873, when its height was increased and it acquired the side arches. It is now the principal gate to the naval base.

HERE IS A VIEW of the long-since vanished Marlborough Row, looking towards the Marlborough Gate, an erstwhile entrance to the dockyard. The year is 1898. The Royal Oak was a beerhouse (see p. 117). There were pubs of that name in Lake Road and, not far away, in Queen Street.

THE GERMAN EMPEROR visited Portsmouth on 11 November 1907 in his royal yacht *Hohenzollern*. Here we see some of the personnel of the squadron of warships that accompanied him leaving the dockyard.

JAPANESE SAILORS OUTSIDE TOWN HALL PORTSMOUTH JULY 12 07

MORA. PHOTO
ELM GROVE
SOUTHSEA

TWO JAPANESE CRUISERS, the *Tsukaba* and *Chitose*, visited Portsmouth on 12–13 July 1907. The officers and men were entertained by the Services and by the Mayor. Here is a group of them outside the Town Hall. The similarity of their uniforms to those of the British Navy is striking.

CORONATION MEMENTO, 1937.
M. & Co.   THE MODEL SHIP, "CORONATION", GUILDHALL SQUARE, PORTSMOUTH.   730

PORTSMOUTH'S CONTRIBUTIONS to the Civic celebrations for the coronation of King George VI included the construction of this model ship in Guildhall Square. The centre-piece of the displays and parades, it was manned by members of the local Sea Cadets who 'lined its rails', in nautical fashion. At night it was spectacularly lit by hundreds of light bulbs.

"VICTORY" SAILING MODEL & WIRELESS CONTROLLED BOA'

THE SAILING MODEL of HMS *Victory* is thought to have been constructed in Portsmouth Dockyard sometime before 1935. Based on a naval launch, she was 60ft in length and manned by a crew who can be seen (white shirted) standing amidships. Photographed while sailing off Clarence Beach, this beautiful vessel is thought to have been neglected and possibly dismantled during the Second World War.

THE SPECTACLE of HM ships entering or leaving Portsmouth Harbour still generates pride in British hearts. In this pre-1939 photograph HMS *Hood* is viewed from Southsea promenade. In May 1941 HMS *Hood* was tragically lost in her epic battle with the German ship *Bismark*.

Portsmouth Harbour.

THE PORT OF PORTSMOUTH FLOATING BRIDGE COMPANY began operating the first regular ferry service across Portsmouth harbour from Point to Gosport on 4 May 1840, using steam-powered chain ferries. The original vessels were called *Victoria* and *Albert*. The former was sold in 1864, to be replaced the following year by *Alexandra*, seen here ...

... AND THE LATTER was replaced in 1892 by *Duchess of York*, illustrated above. The service was sometimes erratic and queues long but, in the era of the horse, such delays were still preferable to the day's journey it took to reach Gosport by road. After the Second World War, the company's financial state became increasingly parlous, and the final service operated on 15 December 1959.

'TOW BOATS', as a means of conveying vehicles and animals to and from the Isle of Wight are known to have been in operation by 1864. By the time the railway companies introduced motor vessels on the service in 1927, there were five. Here is one, loaded with cattle . . .

... AND ANOTHER, laden with cars. Various treasures, including a complete set of fairground gallopers, are reputed to lie somewhere at the bottom of Spithead as a result of mishaps while making the journey. The 'tow boats' drew only 2ft of water, even when fully laden.

SOUTHERN   RAILWAY   MOTOR   VESSEL   "WOOTTON."

PORTSMOUTH — FISHBOURNE   CAR   FERRY   SERVICE.

THE FIRST MOTOR VESSEL on the service was the MV *Fishbourne*, introduced in 1927. She was joined by MV *Wootton* (seen here) in 1928, and by MV *Hilsea* in 1930.

THE PADDLE STEAMER *Duchess of York* is seen beached near Victoria Pier following a collision with the SS *Transporter* on 3 September 1909. There were 400 passengers on the paddle steamer at the time. Fortunately she was close to the shore and the passengers were landed safely, although she took in water and sank shortly after the rescue operation was completed. The SS *Transporter* apparently escaped unscathed.

THIS POSTCARD VIEW of Commercial Road of approximately 1910, shows, on the left, the General Post Office and the Speedwell Hotel before reaching the 'high-rise' Central Hotel on the corner of Edinburgh Road. On the immediate right of the picture is the forecourt of the Portsmouth and Southsea Railway Station. The scaffold-like structure visible on the right-hand skyline is the framework built to receive the telephone lines of the Municipal Exchange which was housed in the building below (see p. 93).

TRAIN SERVICES to Portsmouth (from Brighton) began in October 1847. A line drawing of what purports to be the original station shows a simple train shed with houses immediately to the south. The station had assumed the form shown here by 1876. It was called simply 'Portsmouth' (1847–61); 'Portsmouth and Southsea' (1861–76); 'Portsmouth Town' (1876–1921) and 'Portsmouth and Southsea' again, (1921–to date).

OLD GATES, PORTSMOUTH.

Copyright

KING JAMES' GATE was built in 1687 and originally stood across Broad Street. It was demolished some time after 1874 and re-erected in St Michael's Road, on which site it is seen here. Construction of what is now the Polytechnic's Nuffield Centre necessitated a further removal c. 1949, when the gate found a third home in Burnaby Road.

St. Michaels Road, Portsmouth.

THIS VIEW GIVES A CLEAR INDICATION of the former position of the gate, just opposite the (still standing) offices, originally built for the Board of Guardians, in 1879.

THE AREA OF SOUTHSEA which lies west of the Strand is acknowledged to be the lowest lying on Portsea Island. During the 1960s, massive drainage and sewerage-works were carried out, so relieving the district of the periodic flooding which occurred when prolonged rain accompanied high tides. Houses now occupy the site behind the hoardings and, in the lower picture, high-rise flats have been erected where the single-storey buildings are seen.

GEORGE HANDLEY opened his drapers shop on the corner of Palmerston Road and Portland Road in 1867, and it developed into the best known store in Southsea. The whole area was wrecked in the blitz. Reconstruction resulted in re-alignment of Portland Road, so that Handley's successor, Debenham's, now stands on the corner of Palmerston Road and Osborne Road.

KING'S ROAD (originally Wish Street) was Southsea's first shopping centre, having 20 shops by 1830 and, for many years, outshining Palmerston Road in that respect.

Kings Road, Southsea

ON THE LEFT-HAND SIDE, a little way down, the shop with the sun-blinds is Hide's drapery. In 1882, the young H.G. Wells served an unhappy apprenticeship there. King's Road was badly damaged by bombs in 1941; the rebuilt road is much wider, but now almost entirely residential.

THE NEXT SIX PICTURES show various streets of small houses so typical of Portsmouth before redevelopment and/or the blitz swept them away. Here is Marylebone Street, which led south from Greetham Street. (The whole area was sometimes referred to as Marylebone in the nineteenth century.)

THIS IS COISH LANE, which ran from Clifton Street (off Arundel Street) into Fratton Road.

HERE ARE FRONT AND REAR VIEWS of Town Street, which ran from Upper Church Path to Church Path North. Its north end survives in name.

FINALLY IN THIS SECTION, two streets in old Portsea that both still exist in name: the upper view shows Havant Street and the lower, Butcher Street, as they were more than 50 years ago.

THIS VIEW OF THE GUILDHALL SQUARE C. 1951 is redolent with period detail; the bus and cars, the trolley-wires and associated poles, the bus (formerly tram) shelter in the middle of the square, the policeman in the white coat directing traffic, the Sussex Hotel just visible on the left. Pedestrianization has rendered all this just memories.

A FURTHER WEALTH OF LOST DETAIL can be seen in this pre-war aerial view of the Guildhall area. Working clockwise, note the cupolas and minarets on the Guildhall itself, the railway line branching sharp right leading to the dockyard, Russell Street, the Hippodrome, the Theatre Royal, the back of St Michael's Church, and the old swimming baths, for example. Opinions vary as to whether all the changes that have taken place have been for the better – an *envoi* that can stand for this whole book!

ACKNOWLEDGEMENTS

Our grateful thanks for their assistance in many and various ways are tendered to the following individuals and/or institutions: Mrs S. Quail and the staff of the Portsmouth City Records Office; Mr J. Thorn, Mr A. King and the staff of the local collection of Portsmouth District Central Library; Captain J. Scott of the Museum of Army Flying; Westland Aerospace; Mrs V.L. Carter, Mr B. Ewin, Mr A.N. Gibbs, Mr W. Greer, Mr A. Harris, Mr D.N. Jordan, Mrs J. Lofting, Mr B. Pethybridge, Mr M. Southcott and the late Bill Buckley and, for their help with the manuscript, Mrs P. Castle and Miss L. Schooley.